Keep On Keepin' On

21 Days of Propulsion for the Process

LaToya NaShae

Keep on Keepin' On: 21 Days of Propulsion for the Process
by LaToya NaShae

Cover Art by Elanamarie Fitzgerald
https://isafineartgallery.com/

Printed in the United States of America
ISBN **978-0-578-51952-4**

Dedication

The start of every process has its blind spots and uncertainties. Those initial steps, although governed by faith, are not absent of fear. I am forever grateful to have parents who have supported me even when the road ahead wasn't clear. I "hear" well… and for them, my faith in the voice of my Divine Daddy is enough. Thank you both for always respecting the processes of my life's path.

Hey Friend!

I hope you don't mind if I dive right in. You don't? Good! What is your word??? What is the hard-pressing, God-breathed thing causing you to vacillate between faith-full and doubt-burdened? Ahhh. You see it. You want you. It was promised to you… but where is it? For now, it only seems to exist in the hearts and minds of you and God. Yo! Trust me; I understand all too well the plight you face.

Correct me if I'm wrong, but the dilemma is this: Without vision, normal is palatable. It is sight to see the unseen that causes unrest to stir. Vision triggers a hunger to taste, see, and lay hold of God's goodness. Yaasssss! You know *exactly* what I mean! It is the hope of greater that produces distaste for right now. You know full well that right now is not forever. Still, the future seems so far from your grasp. The promise – however clearly envisioned – seems to be slow in coming. *Wait for it.* If we're being honest (and I hope that we are), you cringe each time the Holy Spirit whispers those three dreaded words. *Wait for it.*

2 And the Lord said to me, "Write my answer on a billboard, large and clear, so that anyone can read it at a glance and rush to tell the others. 3 But these things I plan won't happen right away. **Slowly, steadily, surely, the time approaches when the vision will be fulfilled.** If it seems slow, do not despair, for these things will surely come to pass. Just be patient! They will not be overdue a single day! 4 "Note this: Wicked men trust themselves alone as these Chaldeans do,

1

and fail, but the righteous man trusts in Me and lives! (Habakkuk 2:2-4, TLB)

Friend, trust the process! I know, I know. That is NOT what you wanted to hear. You have *been* trusting. You've *been* making faith declarations. By now you have prayed, fasted, cried, and thrown spiritual fits. Pity parties? We've both had plenty. The Lord our God, who operates outside of time, is not the least bit concerned about our calendars. It is our character that He is after. Through the process patience has its perfect work, causing us to be thorough and complete and without lack. (See James 1:4). Doesn't that sound like God desires more for us than we desire for ourselves? To be true, God has been God for a mighty long time. He doesn't need our help. Only our participation is required for His perfect work to be accomplished in our lives. And here's a hint: Participation, in this regard, is synonymous with surrender. Trust the process, hun.

Although manifestation seems a long time coming, wait for it. *Slowly, steadily, surely, the time approaches when the vision will be fulfilled.* The blessing of God's timing is that it causes fulfilment of His word to be accompanied by wholeness. The fragmented soul struggles to possess the fullness of God's goodness. Roots of rejection and unforgiveness cause wounds to re-open again and again. Insecurity and fear block blessings like a well-trained soccer goalie. Selfishness justifies a life with clinched fists – a life that neither pours out nor receives. Ahh, but the whole soul! Blessed is the one who yields to the process. For in doing so, an inward work of completion produces an outward life of fullness. The process feels like punishment; however, it is far from the likes. As we keep on keepin' on we come to understand that God-size blessings necessitate divine training.

It is through the process that we become equipped. Our capacity must be increased before overflow is experienced. Let us not be naïve in thinking our heavenly Father would bombard us with more without first training us on the level of less. Those who yield to the process of learning to be faithful over a few things will be blessed to rule over many things. (See Matthew 25:21). FACT: We aren't working for God's favor. Grace is a gift to be received, not earned. Nevertheless, faith without works is dead. (James 2:26). To keep on keepin' on is to *actively* wait. There are moves to make and work to be done. Again, our participation is required to see the fulfilment of God's will for our lives. It is our voluntary surrender to the process that shifts God's plan from a possibility to a probability. Vision has been given; now the process must be lived out.

The LORD directs the steps of the godly. He delights in every detail of their lives. (Psalm 37:23, NLT)

Consider the promise spoken over your life. It is as real to you as mine is to me. You have written, revised, and mounted it on your vision board as a reminder of the future to come. Close your eyes. Can you see it? Yes, I know you can. It is as vivid as a memory and almost real enough to be tangible. That thing seems so close yet so far away. The good news and bad news are rolled into one. All that's standing between now and later is the process. Before allowing your countenance to drop, remember that the process is not punishment. *Two are better than one, because they have a good reward for their labor.* (Ecclesiastes 4:9). Be of good cheer, we will walk this out together! Are you in agreement that we will live out this process on one accord?

Your path is not my path nor is my path yours, but our paths have crossed for such a time as this. Rather than fixating on how far away the manifestation seems, let's set our sights on the day-by-day steps of walking out the process.

Father God,

We are Your children. Rather than incessantly pleading for sudden fulfilment, we surrender to Your way, Your order, and Your timing. Lord, as we embark on this 21 day journey, we ask that each day would provide the encouragement needed to propel us to the next day, the next point of instruction, and the next milestone on the road to destiny. In faithfulness You have called us, and in faithfulness You will keep us as Your Word for our lives is performed. We thank You in advance for the blessing of this process. In the name of Jesus we pray. Amen.

Let the journey begin…

WHAT TO EXPECT

Principle

Each principle serves as a compass for our faith. It directs our attention toward God's faithfulness and stabilizes our feet to continue along the path of promise.

Devotional

Here we'll dive into the Word to examine Abraham's process. Together we will seek the Lord's wisdom on how the father of faith's journey applies to our lives.

Propulsion Point

This is the main take away to be gleaned for the day's reading experience.

Discovery

The best way to counter the enemy's lies will always be with God's truth. Each time Satan tempted Jesus in the wilderness, our Lord responded, "It is written…" We will pinpoint the lie that dares to oppose our principles of faith and rebuke them with God's truth.

Declaration

Our world is framed by our words. Speak life! Declare that which the Lord has already spoken. A verse has been provided. Use this as a starting point to craft your personal faith declaration.

PRINCIPLE 1: All is not lost.

Devotional

³¹ And Terah took his son Abram and his grandson Lot, the son of Haran, and his daughter-in-law Sarai, his son Abram's wife, and they went out with them from Ur of the Chaldeans to go to the land of Canaan; and they came to Haran and dwelt there. ³² So the days of Terah were two hundred and five years, and Terah died in Haran. (Genesis 11:31-32)

What is morphs into what was and just like that, the present becomes the past. Shift happens. Those who have lived to see many seasons come to know that normal changes its appearance time and time again. Like the peeling of an onion, faith pulls back the layers of life…and with those layers come the shedding of tears. We struggle to cling to the familiar, but "always" was never promised to last forever. No matter what your "it" may be, just because it has always been doesn't mean it will always be. Change is inevitable. We desperately attempt to hold an unwavering belief that God is good, but in the face of shifting seasons and great loss, we wrestle with unbelief.

Before Abraham became the father of faith, he was Abram, son of Terah. The one who was counted as righteous for his faith in God was first one marked by repetitive loss. It appeared as though he was *always* losing! His brother,

Haran, passed away. His wife, Sarai, was plagued by infertility. Under the direction of his father, Abram left his homeland of Ur of the Chaldeans with his remaining loved ones. He bid farewell to the familiar, no doubt believing that the future would be greater. Surely, things would get better! Then it happened. As if Abram's heart had not taken enough blows, his father died before they reached Canaan. The one who had always guided his steps was no more. He was in unfamiliar territory with little sense of normalcy.

Praise be to God who has mastered the art of crafting masterpieces from our broken pieces! Where we see loss and disappointment, He sees miracle territory. Forget not that He transforms ashes into beauty and exchanges our sorrows for joy. That, my friend, is the God we serve! Loss Lane becomes Promise Parkway to those who dare to believe.

PROPULSION POINT: Experiencing isolated losses – no matter how many – does not define you as a loser.

Discovery

Identify the Lie: The enemy desires for us to remain static and stagnant, unwilling to move and unable to thrive. He wants us to believe that if the thought-to-be key people are no longer in position, the plan falls apart.

Identify the Truth: Living out the will of God requires flexibility. We are to be steadfast and unmovable in our commitment to this life of faith, yet unchained to natural circumstances. Victory is in Jesus. He is the key component in our triumph. No matter how great the call, intimidating the instruction, or devastating the loss, be fully persuaded that success is built into the assignment. Keep that in mind lest rigidity becomes a crippling vice.

Declaration of Faith

Now thanks be to God who always leads us in triumph in Christ, and through us diffuses the fragrance of His knowledge in every place. (II Corinthians 2:14)

PRINCIPLE 2: We are defined by the Divine One.

Devotional

But Sarai was barren; she had no child. (Genesis 11:30).

Barren. Infertile. Fallow. Does it get anymore discouraging than that? Verse thirty pronounces a verdict so finite, so matter-of-fact that all hope seems lost for Abram's lineage if it is to be dependent on Sarai. The thing expected to be naturally occurring proved to be a stumbling block. Dreams of birthing an heir and motherhood were shattered by the dreaded b-word. Barrenness.

Thankfully, the labels to which we are subjected during the process do not dictate our destiny. Before time had the chance to tick or tock, the Father knew the thoughts He had toward Abram and Sarai. At the sound of His voice, their names were changed. Their situation was redefined.

Abraham was to be the father of many nations, and Sarah would provide the birth canal through which the foretold seed of promise would enter the world. As for us, the Lord's thoughts toward us are no less grand. We are children of faith - those promised to Abraham in the days of old, destined to live out the Blessing.

Barren. Broken. Belittled. Bastard. Battered. Betrayed. No matter your b-word, my b-word, or any other negative word beginning with any other letter, the Lord our God has spoken. It is His decree that shall be. Labels are temporary;

God's Word is irrefutable. We are His workmanship. We are fearfully and wonderfully made in His likeness. Be not dismayed by the process' labels. Together, we have committed to entrusting our lives to the hands of the Potter. "Right now is not forever," thus says the Author and Finisher of our faith.

PROPULSION POINT: Where you are doesn't define who you are. Your identity rests in WHOSE you are.

Discovery
Identify the Lie: Fruitfulness is not for you.

Identify the Truth: Be fruitful; multiply; have dominion. According to the blessing spoken over man and woman in Genesis 1:28, productivity and authority are inherent to our nature. Whether it is our gifts, talents, wisdom, or gene pool, multiplication is the expectation. Everything that God initiates He does in seed form. There is more to you than that which currently exists. Multiplication is for you.

Declaration
Everyone who is called by My name, whom I have created for My glory; I have formed him, yes, I have made him. (Isaiah 43:7)

PRINCIPLE 3: Every process is initiated by a promise.

Devotional

Now the LORD had said to Abram: "Get out of your country, from your family and from your father's house, to a land that I will show you. ² I will make you a great nation; I will bless you and make your name great, and you shall be a blessing. ³ I will bless those who bless you, and I will curse him who curses you, and in you all the families of the earth shall be blessed." (Genesis 12:1-3)

Wouldn't it be lovely to receive the promise then, BOOM, instantly experience manifestation? Occasionally such is the case, but more often than not the promise initiates a process whose duration is known by God while remaining a mystery to us. Our natural inclination is to become so focused on expectation that the passing of days, weeks, months, and in some cases years serves as a nagging point of frustration.

Shake off the temptation to doubt! You heard what you heard. God said what He said. Believe that! Wait for the vision although it tarries. You heard the Word of the Lord spoken over your life, and the Word of the Lord does not return void. What is to be done in the interim?

Promises are partnered with instruction. Abram had to separate himself from his heritage before God would bestow his inheritance. What instruction have you been given? What stone has been left unturned? Faith without works is dead.

True expectation is preceded by preparation. Do the part that rests under your authority. Your peace is in trusting that God has handled His piece.

Propulsion Point: The road to destiny is lined with directives. Do them.

Discovery

Identify the Lie: Details don't matter. If I believe, I will receive.

Identify the Truth: We are called to be active participants in the process of faith. The Lord directs the steps of those who trust Him, causing us to walk in the direction of His promises. He orders our steps in a way that directs us toward rather than derails us from destiny.

Declaration

Seek His will in all you do, and He will show you which path to take. (Proverbs 3:6, NLT)

PRINCIPLE 4: It's never too late for a new thing.

Devotional

[4] So Abram departed as the LORD had spoken to him, and Lot went with him. And Abram was seventy-five years old when he departed from Haran. (Genesis 12:4)

The infamous "they", whoever they may be, is notorious for boxing us in with inferiority complexes. We are made to believe that we are too much of this or not enough of that to embark on a new journey. While we go to war within ourselves, the world keeps turning. Time stands still for no one, not even those wrestling with insecurities. As the battle with our individual enemies (aka the inner you and inner me) wages on, the calendar turns page after page.

Oh but bay-bee, the God we serve is in no way bound by time! He breaks down barriers. The Lord our God pays no mind to the passing of seconds, minutes or decades for that matter. Just as an entire dry bone army was raised to life by His Word, so shall the turnaround be for you and me. The promise isn't dead; it is simply in need of revival.

Too much time has passed? Time is redeemed for those who act in accordance with that which the Lord has spoken. As Evangelist Linden Ravenhill so wisely stated, "Opportunities of a lifetime must be seized within the lifetime of the opportunity." The call to depart was spoken into Abram's present rather than his past. Although it came when

19

he was advanced in years, the instruction came at the appointed time. Whatever we are called to in this season is for this season. Friends, let us boldly walk on into the new thing knowing that it is for right now.

PROPULSION POINT: You are just right to step into the new thing.

Discovery

Identify the Lie: Delays and mistakes have caused too much time to be wasted.

Identify the Truth: Isaiah 43:19 declares that God will do a new thing. Roads will be made through the wilderness and rivers will spring up in the desert. No place is too desolate or depleted for our God. With Him ALL THINGS are possible. He is well able to do a new thing in the lives of you and me.

Declaration

4 Again He said to me, "Prophesy to these bones, and say to them, 'O dry bones, hear the word of the LORD! 5 Thus says the Lord GOD to these bones: "Surely I will cause breath to enter into you, and you shall live. 6 I will put sinews on you and bring flesh upon you, cover you with skin and put breath in you; and you shall live. Then you shall know that I am the LORD.' " (Ezekiel 37:4-6)

PRINCIPLE 5: What's for you isn't just about you.

Devotional

[6] Abram passed through the land to the place of Shechem, as far as the terebinth tree of Moreh. And the Canaanites were then in the land. [7] Then the LORD appeared to Abram and said, "To your descendants I will give this land." And there he built an altar to the LORD, who had appeared to him. (Genesis 12:6-7)

Consider the generational impact of present day choices. Decisions made by you and I touch lives far beyond ours. The consequences - be they blessings or curses - spread far and reach wide. Choose life. As we choose the path of light and truth and righteousness the blessed way is paved for future generations.

Abraham is the father of faith, and we are his seed. In the same manner, our descendants are marked by our faith or lack thereof. Where we go our seed shall follow. Selfishness must have no place in our decision making. Let us walk as if we are leading our children's children into newness. If we would pause to look through the lens of faith and see beyond the temptation of instant gratification, we would see that where we go they are likely to follow. So, stretch a little further. Walk it out a little longer. To step into our set place of promise requires walking the path of obedience.

In the words of renowned author and speaker Dr. Cindy Trimm, "An inheritance is what you leave; a legacy is who you leave." The process of each promise steadies the foundation of your legacy. Those whom you leave and I leave are also those whom we will have led. I pray that as they trustingly follow us we would follow faithfully after Christ.

PROPULSION POINT: Obedience is a seed that continues to produce fruit for generations to come.

Discovery

Identify the Lie: Your life, your decisions, and your consequences are just that – YOURS. The only person impacted by the repercussions of your actions is you.

Identify the Truth: The result of forty-two generations of imperfect people displaying exemplary faith was Christ's birth. He was the foretold one of the Old Testament and the promise-fulfilled of the New Testament. The decisions of each generation mattered. Abraham, Isaac, Jacob, Ruth, Rahab, David, Mary and Joseph – the choices they made had a generational impact. As do ours. Generational blessings are put in place and propelled in the same manner as generational curses. Decisions matter.

Declaration

[14] "So now: Fear GOD. Worship Him in total commitment. Get rid of the gods your ancestors worshiped on the far side of The River (the Euphrates) and in Egypt. You, worship GOD. [15] "If you decide that it's a bad thing to worship GOD, then choose a god you'd rather serve—and do it today. Choose one of the gods your ancestors worshiped from the country beyond The River, or one of the gods of the Amorites, on whose land you're now living. As for me and my family, we'll worship GOD." (Joshua 24:14-15, The Message)

PRINCIPLE 6: Some battles fought will not be personal.

Devotional

[11] Then they took all the goods of Sodom and Gomorrah, and all their provisions, and went their way. [12] They also took Lot, Abram's brother's son who dwelt in Sodom, and his goods, and departed. [13] Then one who had escaped came and told Abram the Hebrew, for he dwelt by the terebinth trees of Mamre the Amorite, brother of Eshcol and brother of Aner; and they were allies with Abram. [14] Now when Abram heard that his brother was taken captive, he armed his three hundred and eighteen trained servants who were born in his own house, and went in pursuit as far as Dan. (Genesis 14:11-14)

Lot was taken captive due to being in the wrong place at the wrong time. Dwelling in the region of Sodom and Gomorrah was *his* choice. The well-watered plain of Jordan was beautiful and suitable for prosperous living, or so he thought. All that glitters ain't gold! His place of habitation turned out to be a beautiful problem – a tussle which he was not equipped to fight alone.

We who are strong are called to bear the infirmities of the weak. (See Romans 15:1). Along the path of promise we will be called to wars that we did not incite because sincere love is displayed in action and not word alone. Who will be the one to walk with her best friend as she severs the soul tie of a relationship not ordained by God? Who will answer the 1 am call of that co-worker who is contemplating suicide? For whom will we intercede? For whom will we go to war? Once upon a time, before you or I took form in our mothers' wombs, the Son of God defeated sin and death for us. Victory was won on our behalf. Love compels us to lead others to a place of victory as well.

PROPULSION POINT: Extend mercy as you have received mercy.

Discovery

Identify the Lie: Their problem is *their* problem.

Identify the Truth: Beloved, if God so loved us, we also ought to love one another. (I John 4:11). Encompassed within the love of God is an undeniable element of sacrifice. The Father gave the Son as ransom for our sins. The Son bore the weight of our wrongs as He hung on the Cross. Love inconveniences itself for the sake of others. Love laced with unshaken comfort needs to be called into question.

Declaration

⁴ But God, who is rich in mercy, because of His great love with which He loved us, ⁵ even when we were dead in trespasses, made us alive together with Christ (by grace you have been saved). (Ephesians 2:4-5)

PRINCIPLE 7: Revelation comes incrementally.

Devotional

² But Abram said, "Lord GOD, what will You give me, seeing I go childless, and the heir of my house is Eliezer of Damascus?" ³ Then Abram said, "Look, You have given me no offspring; indeed, one born in my house is my heir!" ⁴ And behold, the word of the LORD came to him, saying, "This one shall not be your heir, but one who will come from your own body shall be your heir." ⁵ Then He brought him outside and said, "Look now toward heaven, and count the stars if you are able to number them." And He said to him, "So shall your descendants be." ⁶ And he believed in the LORD, and He accounted it to him for righteousness. (Genesis 15:2-6)

Piece by piece, revelation is received. Prayer by prayer, vision takes shape. Let us find contentment in the pace at which the Father's blueprint is revealed. Too much too soon is not His way. For everything – every season, every promise, and every process – there is a time, pace, and rhythm. Unfortunately, it is not only "slow" manifestation that works our nerves. Not knowing the how by which things will take place is often just as frustrating. With loving kindness the Lord spoon feeds us morsels of His masterpiece in the making. We proclaim to trust the works of His hands, but let us equally trust in every grip, every flex, and every prod of His foreknowing fingers. Movement by movement, the Potter's perfect work is being performed.

Lean in and listen. Hear. Breathe. Now, lean in again. The One who formed us is well able to clear up our misconceptions. Maybe, just maybe, our minds are moving at a pace that exceeds how God has called understanding to be known. Abram received the promise of his name being made great; by the word of the Lord he would become a great nation. But what does that *look* like? Would his legacy be left in the hands of someone who did not come from his loins? No, that wasn't to be the case at all. The promises of God are often layered. Those layers are pulled back and understood as we walk in union with His Spirit. It is not enough to just trust the process; we must trust the speed at which understanding for each level is granted.

PROPULSION POINT: Commit by faith; understanding will follow.

Discovery

Identify the Lie: The Lord provides the vision, but it is our duty to determine the path.

Identify the Truth: Listen to the Father's instruction; pay attention and understanding will be made known. (See Proverbs 4:1). It is the Lord who orders our steps. His voice leads us into destiny.

Declaration

[5] Trust in the LORD with all your heart, and lean not on your own understanding; [6] in all your ways acknowledge Him, and He shall direct your paths. (Proverbs 3:5-6)

PRINCIPLE 8: Belief necessitates a journey.

Devotional

And he believed in the LORD, and He accounted it to him for righteousness. (Genesis 15:6)

Abram stood on what he believed despite what he knew. The opposing factors of his faith were blaring reminders of reality. Time was not on his side. Biology's say-so seemed like a final verdict. In no way were God's words lining up with the facts. Nevertheless, the Lord had spoken, and Abram CHOSE to believe.

In the words of the late Dr. Myles Munroe, "When you don't know where you're going, any road will do." Conversely, *narrow is the gate and difficult is the way which leads to life, and there are few who find it.* (Matthew 7:14). The Lord's prescribed path for us is both specific and strategic, and it often conflicts with the norm. Reality's details do not override God's divinity.

We who claim ownership over our God-breathed promises embark on a journey of faith that few dare to tread. For the world seeing dictates belief. To those of us within the household of faith, we see as a result of having heard. Are you a believer?

PROPULSION POINT: Faith is a stabilizing force.

Discovery

Identify the Lie: It is IMPOSSIBLE to remain in faith for the impossible!

Identify the Truth: Faith is *for* the impossible! We serve a God who specializes in encompassing our natural with His super. His past is our future. The Spirit leads us in a way prepared before one foot of yours or mine was placed in front of the other. The expectation is for us to remain in faith without doubting because He who calls us is faithful and His Word is unfailing.

Declaration

[9] "For as the heavens are higher than the earth, so are My ways higher than your ways, and My thoughts than your thoughts. [10] "For as the rain comes down, and the snow from heaven, and do not return there, but water the earth, and make it bring forth and bud, that it may give seed to the sower and bread to the eater, [11] so shall My word be that goes forth from My mouth; it shall not return to Me void, but it shall accomplish what I please, and it shall prosper in the thing for which I sent it. (Isaiah 55:9-11)

PRINCIPLE 9: The I Am who called you is the I AM who will guide and keep you.

Devotional

Then He said to him, "I am the LORD, who brought you out of Ur of the Chaldeans, to give you this land to inherit it." (Genesis 15:7)

Consistency is such a beautiful thing, isn't it? Travis Greene sang the words, "Who You were is who You are; who You are is who You will always be." The Mighty One of Heaven is our unchanging way-maker and peace-giver. Times, seasons, and even people will inevitably change to some degree, but there is no shadow of turning in His character. Who He is, He shall always be. May our hearts be stilled and our spirits comforted. It is this assurance that should firmly plant our feet on the process' path. Because of this, we need not fear telling sight to have a seat. Vision fueled by faith guides our feet for this expedition.

My dear, the One who called you is the One leading you. The One leading you is the One who is faithful to fulfill **every single word** spoken over your life. Ayyye! You can hallelujah on that! He brought you out of yesterday to lead you boldly into tomorrow. As for today, love, trust Him in the middle.

PROPULSION POINT: I AM is consistently, faithfully present.

Discovery
Identify the Lie: God will periodically pull back to see if we will sink or swim in the sea of faith.

Identify the Truth: Jesus is The Way, The Truth, and The Life. It is by Him that we enter into the Father's presence. (John 14:6) It is through Him that we are granted access to God's riches – both tangible and intangible. (See Philippians 4:19) We will never be forsaken, forgotten, or led astray by The Way. That is the Truth as declared by The Life. Proximity is determined by us, not I AM.

Declaration
30 When you are in distress, and all these things come upon you in the latter days, when you turn to the LORD your God and obey His voice 31 (for the LORD your God is a merciful God), He will not forsake you nor destroy you, nor forget the covenant of your fathers which He swore to them. (Deuteronomy 4:30-31)

PRINCIPLE 10: Within the promise are valleys as well as mountaintops.

Devotional

[13] Then He said to Abram: "Know certainly that your descendants will be strangers in a land that is not theirs, and will serve them, and they will afflict them four hundred years. [14] And also the nation whom they serve I will judge; afterward they shall come out with great possessions. (Genesis 15:13-14)

The bad news is trouble will come. The good news is trials and tribulations have an expiration date. Breathe, boo! Even when all is not well, God is causing all things – the good, the bad, and the not so pretty – to work together for our good. (See Romans 8:28) Turnaround lies ahead. We *have* to keep on keepin' on!

On the road to greater, mishaps and misfortunes will occur. We will find ourselves in unfamiliar territory – unsure of where we are and uncertain of how to proceed. Let us be fully persuaded that God is no less faithful during rough patches. Valleys are not the time for drawing back but rather for pressing in. Come what may, the just shall live by faith. (See Hebrews 10:38) Friend, we are the just.

PROPULSION POINT: Valleys do not nullify the promise.

Discovery

Identify the Lie: Hard times are proof that the mark was completely missed.

Identify the Truth: According to Ecclesiastes chapter 3, there is a time for everything, including a time to break down and a time to build up. Throughout life, wrong mindsets and bad habits are built up by experiences and wrong teaching. Whether a trial is an attack of the enemy or the result of our missteps, they are always prime opportunity for the tearing down of wrong paradigms and the building up of new, faith-based belief systems. Despise not the tough time. Our God upcycles. Trials entrusted to Him will be used for our good and His glory.

Declaration

But as for you, you meant evil against me; but God meant it for good, in order to bring it about as it is this day, to save many people alive. (Genesis 50:20)

PRINCIPLE 11: The ones who love you are not guaranteed to rightly guide you.

Devotional

[1]Now Sarai, Abram's wife, had borne him no children. And she had an Egyptian maidservant whose name was Hagar. [2]So Sarai said to Abram, "See now, the Lord has restrained me from bearing children. Please, go in to my maid; perhaps I shall obtain children by her." And Abram heeded the voice of Sarai. (Genesis 16:1-2)

Y'all, Abe fell for the okie-doke. Wait though. We need not be too quick to judge him. You see, in the beginning was the Word; it was with God and it was God. (John 1:1). However, the Bible has not always been. Abram did not have the luxury of flipping through the pages of Hebrews chapter 11 to gain insight on operating by faith as we do. In his quest to become a father, he could not have fathomed that he would one day be known as the father of faith. Abram heeded the words of the one he loved versus trusting the One who lovingly called him out of darkness into marvelous light. Truth be told, we are guilty of having done the same thing a time or two.

Surely, Sarai felt as though the end would justify the means. Abram needed an heir for the promise of God to be fulfilled. Why not offer her counsel to serve as a catalyst for the process? Hun, in the Kingdom of God the means always matter. The will of God consists of His way, His order, and His timing. Our obedience rather than our help is what the Lord desires. It is by adhering to the molding and shaping of the Potter that promise and purpose are lived out.

PROPULSION POINT: Advice not in alignment with the promise must be dismissed.

Discovery

Identify the Lie: Well-intentioned counsel causes no harm.

Identify the Truth: There is wisdom in a multitude of counselors. This holds true when the counselors have the mind of Christ, for in their words are truth and righteousness. Wise counselors will assure you that although the promise tarries, God withholds no good thing from those who walk uprightly. (See Psalm 84:11)

Declaration

Dear friends, do not believe everyone who claims to speak by the Spirit. You must test them to see if the spirit they have comes from God. For there are many false prophets in the world. (I John 4:1)

PRINCIPLE 12: Hasty decisions produce seeds of conflict.

Devotional

[11] And the Angel of the LORD said to her: "Behold, you are with child, and you shall bear a son. You shall call his name Ishmael, because the LORD has heard your affliction. [12] He shall be a wild man; his hand shall be against every man, and every man's hand against him. And he shall dwell in the presence of all his brethren." (Genesis 16:11-12)

Cause and effect, actions and consequences, sowing and reaping – no matter the name, the principle holds true. As we sow so shall we reap. As promised by Genesis 8:22, as long as the earth remains, so will seedtime and harvest. FACT: Thoughts, words, and actions are seed types.

The seed of Abram's hasty decision was Ishmael; the fruit of Ishmael continues to be generational strife. By attempting to take the pieces of God's promise into his hands, Abram produced a son whose descendants would forever be without peace. Ishmael was destined to dwell in the presence of his brothers; therefore, compromise and promise would permanently be at odds.

PROPULSION POINT: Things created in the flesh contend with the things created by the Spirit.

Discovery

Identify the Lie: Sin that is forgiven works to produce the will of God.

Identify the Truth: The will of God is performed in spite of our sin not in conjunction with it. Righteousness is to have no fellowship with lawlessness nor should light commune with darkness. (See II Corinthians 6:14). The standard set for the people are God is the standard exemplified by the character of God. When we attempt to partner duelling realities, the resulting ramifications can have negative, multi-generational impact.

Declaration

[16] I say then: Walk in the Spirit, and you shall not fulfill the lust of the flesh. [17] For the flesh lusts against the Spirit, and the Spirit against the flesh; and these are contrary to one another, so that you do not do the things that you wish. (Galatians 5:16-17)

PRINCIPLE 13: God speaks of what shall be rather than what we have done.

Devotional

[4] "As for Me, behold, My covenant is with you, and you shall be a father of many nations. [5] No longer shall your name be called Abram, but your name shall be Abraham; for I have made you a father of many nations. [6] I will make you exceedingly fruitful, and I will make nations of you, and kings shall come from you. (Genesis 17:4-5)

The world sees us as we are; God calls us as we shall be. Our heavenly Father endows us with a cleansed heart and a renewed mind, but He doesn't stop there. The Lord our God calls us sons and daughters; He calls us His workmanship and a chosen generation. Why all the divine name-calling? He knows full well that names produce identity and identity paves the way to destiny. Abram was a man of many sorrows and losses but Abraham? Hunny, Abraham was ordained to be blessed beyond measure and abundantly fruitful! Old things passed away when God declared his new name.

We serve a forward-speaking God. Praise Him! We can't keep looking over our shoulders, mulling over what could have been or what we should not have done. His voice propels us into the future rather than cementing us in the past. Shhh. Listen. Do you hear it? He's calling your name.

He is beckoning you and me into our respective places of promise.

PROPULSION POINT: God is doing a new thing in, through, and for you.

Discovery

Identify the Lie: The past nullifies the promise.

Identify the Truth: Where sin abounds, grace abounds more. (Romans 5:20), There is nothing – absolutely nothing – the Blood of Jesus cannot overcome. It cleanses us from all unrighteousness. By Christ, we are made new. In Him we experience a new identity.

Declaration

Therefore, if anyone is in Christ, he is a new creation; old things have passed away; behold, all things have become new. (II Corinthians 5:17)

PRINCIPLE 14: The Word works on your behalf.

Devotional

[15]Then God said to Abraham, "As for Sarai your wife, you shall not call her name Sarai, but Sarah shall be her name. [16]And I will bless her and also give you a son by her; then I will bless her, and she shall be a mother of nations; kings of peoples shall be from her. (Genesis 17:15-16)

In the beginning, God spoke and every word uttered caused His intentions to manifest. His voice still produces. It still takes nothing and creates something. Today… I mean, right now … the Word still delivers, heals, and restores. Yaassss! Step aside Sarai; Sarah has some birthing to do. And so do you.

Speak, friend! The Lord has given you a word. It is tucked away in your heart, but now is the time for release. Speak to your life's barren places. Let faith arise! Call that thing to fruition! You are who God says you are. You shall be and do according to His preordained plan for your life. Speak your promise, boo! I'll be speaking mine too.

PROPULSION POINT: The Word works; work the Word.

Discovery

Identify the Lie: It's too late.

Identify the Truth: It ain't over until God says it's over! We are talking about the One who hung the stars and set the earth on its axis. Nothing is too hard for God. Time is not an opponent of His perfect will. David said, "I have been young, and now am old, yet I have not seen the righteous forsaken, nor his descendants begging bread. (Psalm 37:25) The Lord won't fail in your lifetime… or ever. No matter how long it's been, maintain your confession.

Declaration

So shall My word be that goes forth from My mouth; it shall not return to Me void, but it shall accomplish what I please, and it shall prosper in the thing for which I sent it. (Isaiah 55:11)

PRINCIPLE 15: Compromise divides the heart.

Devotional

[17] Then Abraham fell on his face and laughed, and said in his heart, "Shall a child be born to a man who is one hundred years old? And shall Sarah, who is ninety years old, bear a child?" [18] And Abraham said to God, "Oh, that Ishmael might live before You!" [19] Then God said: "No, Sarah your wife shall bear you a son, and you shall call his name Isaac; I will establish My covenant with him for an everlasting covenant, and with his descendants after him. (Genesis 17:17-19)

A man's heart determines his speech. (Matthew 12:34, TLB). Words of desperation are the overflow of a divided heart. Abraham desperately desired the promise of God, but his emotions were in conflict with the timing of God's method. Ishmael was no less his son; he was alive and well and capable of carrying out his legacy. Or so it seemed from a natural perspective. The qualification was not only that the seed of promise come from Abraham's loins but also that he come from Sarah's womb. Ishmael was Abraham's first son; however, Isaac was God's chosen one.

Stepping outside of the Lord's will causes the heart to become entangled in situations that cloud our judgment and redirect our focus. Efforts are made to camouflage compromise as ordained promises. Internally, a war wages as we waver between our present wants and the pending manifestation of God's promise. When attempting to produce the God-thing in a human way, heartbreaking conflict is sure to follow.

PROPULSION POINT: Compromise leads to conflict.

Discovery

Identify the Lie: God blessed Ishmael; He will bless your compromise too.

Identify the Truth: [13] Yet I will also make a nation of the son of the bondwoman, because he is your seed." [14] So Abraham rose early in the morning, and took bread and a skin of water; and putting it on her shoulder, he gave it and the boy to Hagar, and sent her away. Then she departed and wandered in the Wilderness of Beersheba. (Genesis 21:13-14)

God did indeed bless Ishmael because he was Abraham's seed. Nevertheless, this same blessed boy was sent into the wilderness because his presence was a point of contention rather than the product of covenant. Emotion cannot be removed from the message. Compromise has heartbreaking consequences.

Declaration

Wait on the LORD; be of good courage, and He shall strengthen your heart; wait, I say, on the LORD! (Psalm 27:14)

PRINCIPLE 16: Faith is the force that moves God.
Devotional

¹¹ Now Abraham and Sarah were old, well advanced in age; and Sarah had passed the age of childbearing. ¹² Therefore Sarah laughed within herself, saying, "After I have grown old, shall I have pleasure, my lord being old also?" ¹³ And the LORD said to Abraham, "Why did Sarah laugh, saying, 'Shall I surely bear a child, since I am old?' ¹⁴ Is anything too hard for the LORD? At the appointed time I will return to you, according to the time of life, and Sarah shall have a son." (Genesis 18:11-14)

I will return to you at the appointed time. The appointed time??? Let Sarah tell it, that time had long passed. Abraham wasn't what he used to be, and Aunt Flow's monthly visits were a distant memory. Still, God spoke of a time to come. No matter what time had to say, the promise would be fulfilled.

Present circumstances create no pressure for God to perform "suddenlies". Although He is fully capable of changing our lives in an instant, would microwaved miracles build our faith? Would we be prepared for the weight of an instantaneous, life-altering blessing? No and no. The aim of the Father is not to enable spiritual infants but to cultivate faith-filled sons and daughters. Time is a requirement, not a punishment. Our fear cannot force His hand. Disbelief will not coerce Him into speeding up the process' pace. It is faith that pleases the Lord; faith is the force that moves Him.

PROPULSION POINT: Time has no bearing on God's power.

Discovery

Identify the Lie: Moves of God come to disprove our doubt.

Identify the Truth: But without faith it is impossible to please Him, for he who comes to God must believe that He is, and that He is a rewarder of those who diligently seek Him. (Hebrews 11:6). To see the fulfillment of God's promise, believe His Word. Trust that His faithfulness endures throughout the ages. Faith calls heaven's realities to earth. Be it unto you – whatever your promise may be – according to your faith, not fear.

Declaration

Being confident of this very thing, that He who has begun a good work in you will complete it until the day of Jesus Christ. (Philippians 1:6)

PRINCIPLE 17: The Lord's will is made known to those who walk with Him.

Devotional

¹⁶ Then the men got up from there, and looked toward Sodom, and Abraham walked with them to send them on the way. ¹⁷ The LORD said, "Shall I keep secret from Abraham [My friend and servant] what I am going to do, ¹⁸ since Abraham is destined to become a great and mighty nation, and all the nations of the earth will be blessed through him?¹⁹ For I have known (chosen, acknowledged) him [as My own], so that he may teach and command his children and [the sons of] his household after him to keep the way of the LORD by doing what is righteous and just, so that the LORD may bring upon Abraham what He has promised him." (Genesis 18:16-19, Amplified)

How shallow it is to bypass the face of God in search of His hand! In His presence is fullness of joy and pleasures forevermore, and it doesn't end there. (See Psalm 16:11) As we nestle into the Secret Place, we find that provision does not have to be chased down, mysteries do not remain a secret, and protection is in the shelter of His wings. As we abide in His presence, we become known to Him and Him to us. The One we serve is our Father, Friend, and Fortress.

PROPULSION POINT: To walk with God is to be intimately known by God and to receive personal revelation regarding His will.

Discovery
Identify the Lie: God is too vast to be concerned with personally connecting with His people.

Identify the Truth: Behold, I stand at the door and knock. If anyone hears My voice and opens the door, I will come in to him and dine with him, and he with Me. (Revelation 3:20). May we never downplay Christ choosing to wrap His deity in humanity for the purpose of removing the divide between us and the Father. It is by and through God the Son that we have access to God the Father. Since the fall of man, the Godhead's goal has been to reconcile us to the Lord. His heart's desire is that we would choose to walk with Him and be known by Him as friend.

Declaration
But seek first the kingdom of God and His righteousness, and all these things shall be added to you. (Matthew 6:33)

PRINCIPLE 18: Be mindful not to neglect the power of intercession while in process.

Devotional

[32] Then [Abraham] said, "Let not the Lord be angry, and I will speak but once more: Suppose ten should be found there?" And He said, "I will not destroy it for the sake of ten." [33] So the LORD went His way as soon as He had finished speaking with Abraham, and Abraham returned to his place. (Genesis 18:32-33) ... And it came to pass, when God destroyed the cities of the plain, that God remembered Abraham, and sent Lot out of the midst of the overthrow, when He overthrew the cities in which Lot had dwelt. (Genesis 19:29)

Sweetie, I understand. Trust me. You and I both have our valleys to cross and mountains to climb. Remaining in faith for the fulfillment of that which has been promised requires focus. But as we look to the hills from whence cometh our help, let us also lift up our voices in prayer for those who are going through too.

Poor Lot; bless his whole heart! Once again he was in a bind, and once again Uncle Abraham was on the lookout. God spared Lot because He remembered Abraham. Surely, we have received mercy as a result of those to whom we are connected. Could it be that our relationship with the Almighty also serves as a conduit through which mercy flows into the lives of individuals joined to us as well? Of course!

The goal of the enemy is to have us so consumed with our issues that we fail to intercede on behalf the weary, broken, and at risk. Yield not to temptation! Our faith is strong enough to stretch outward. We who are strong ought to bear the infirmities of the weak. (Romans 15:1, KJV). Sometimes the best way to step in is to kneel down. Let us pray...

PROPULSION POINT: We must remember to prioritize praying for those who are in process as well.

Discovery

Identify the Lie: People are solely responsible for praying for themselves.

Identify the Truth: As Christians we are called to be Christ-like. Christ interceded for us on earth and now does so at the right hand of God in heaven. (See Romans 8:34)

We are in the world to be salt and light. We have not been abandoned but rather positioned to make an impact. Intercession touches the lives of those around us. As Christ covers us, so shall we cover others in His name and by His Spirit.

Declaration

[15] I do not pray that You should take them out of the world, but that You should keep them from the evil one. [16] They are not of the world, just as I am not of the world. [17] Sanctify them by Your truth. Your word is truth. [18] As You sent Me into the world, I also have sent them into the world. (John 17:15-18)

PRINCIPLE 19: Promises manifest at their appointed time.

Devotional

¹ the LORD visited Sarah as He had said, and the LORD did for Sarah as He had spoken. ² For Sarah conceived and bore Abraham a son in his old age, at the set time of which God had spoken to him. ³ And Abraham called the name of his son who was born to him—whom Sarah bore to him—Isaac. (Genesis 21:1-3)

Pause. Rewind. *The Lord visited Sarah AS HE HAD SAID, and the Lord did for Sarah AS HE HAD SPOKEN.* Y'all, He said what He said! The struggle gets real, but child of God – by the Spirit of God within you who is your peace – stay the course. Abraham wasn't perfect and Sarah battled internally to believe; yet, they persevered towards the promise. What's stopping us from doing the same?

When present conditions dare to threaten our faith, we must revisit the promise. What did God say? Meditate on the Word. The same God who enabled Moses to part the Red Sea, equipped Nehemiah to rebuild the wall, and impregnated Mary with our Messiah is the same God who is propelling you through the process for the birthing of a new thing. Hunny, He said what He said. See it – as in envision it – before you see it, and surely you will see it. The promise will materialize at the appointed time.

PROPULSION POINT: God is faithful to do what He said He will do.

Discovery

Identify the Lie: It's too late.

Identify the Truth: [39] When He came in, He said to them, "Why make this commotion and weep? The child is not dead, but sleeping." [40] And they ridiculed Him. But when He had put them all outside, He took the father and the mother of the child, and those who were with Him, and entered where the child was lying. [41] Then He took the child by the hand, and said to her, "Talitha, cumi," which is translated, "Little girl, I say to you, arise." [42] Immediately the girl arose and walked, for she was twelve years of age. (Mark 5:39-42)

Looks can be deceiving. This is precisely why we walk by faith and not sight. (II Corinthians 5:7). The Bread of Life serves as nourishment to seemingly dead things. When the Lord deems a thing as not dead or not over, know that restoration is in the works. His Word prospers in the thing that it was sent to do… at the time it was sent to do it.

Declaration

The smallest family shall multiply into a clan; the tiny group shall be a mighty nation. I, the Lord, will bring it all to pass when it is time. (Isaiah 60:22, TLB)

PRINCIPLE 20: Beware idolatry.

Declaration

² Then He said, "Take now your son, your only son Isaac, whom you love, and go to the land of Moriah, and offer him there as a burnt offering on one of the mountains of which I shall tell you."

³ So Abraham rose early in the morning and saddled his donkey, and took two of his young men with him, and Isaac his son; and he split the wood for the burnt offering, and arose and went to the place of which God had told him. (Genesis 22:2-4)

How dare God expect Abraham to offer his son as a sacrifice! Oh wait. Hmm. That sounds familiar, right? *For God so loved the world that He gave His only begotten Son, that whoever believes in Him should not perish but have everlasting life.* (John 3:16). Isn't it something how God never requires anything of us that He is not willing to do Himself? Where there is love, there is sacrifice. Furthermore, to love God is to obey Him. (See John 14:15).

Where the Spirit of the Lord is, there is freedom. (II Corinthians 3:17). Bondage enters when we become so fixated on finally seeing the fulfillment of the thing that we have prayed, cried, and fasted for that we forget the Father.

Without intentional awareness, lingering enthusiasm over the manifested word can morph into idolatry. The Lord our God is a jealous God. He shall have no noun – person, place, thing, or idea – ruling His place on the throne of our hearts.

For you shall not worship any other god; for the LORD, whose name is Jealous, is a jealous (impassioned) God [demanding what is rightfully and uniquely His]. (Exodus 34:14, Amplified).

PROPULSION POINT: Live before God with an open hand – ready to receive and willing to offer back.

Discovery

Identify the Lie: God is out here playing games with this giving and taking!

Identify the Truth: [3] Then the LORD sent this message through the prophet Haggai: [4] "Why are you living in luxurious houses while my house lies in ruins? [5] This is what the LORD of Heaven's Armies says: Look at what's happening to you! [6] You have planted much but harvest little. You eat but are not satisfied. You drink but are still thirsty. You put on clothes but cannot keep warm. Your wages disappear as though you were putting them in pockets filled with holes! (Haggai 1:3-6, NLT)

It is never the will of God that we worship anything above

Him. Length of days is in loving Him. Destruction comes when the gift is exalted above the Giver. Our hearts are tried to ensure that we rightly position blessings under the Blesser.

Declaration

[19] "Today I have given you the choice between life and death, between blessings and curses. Now I call on heaven and earth to witness the choice you make. Oh, that you would choose life, so that you and your descendants might live! [20] You can make this choice by loving the LORD your God, obeying him, and committing yourself firmly to him. This is the key to your life. And if you love and obey the LORD, you will live long in the land the LORD swore to give your ancestors Abraham, Isaac, and Jacob." (Deuteronomy 30:19-20, NLT)

PRINCIPLE 21: Clarity will come.

Devotional

[15] Then the Angel of the LORD called to Abraham a second time out of heaven, [16] and said: "By Myself I have sworn, says the LORD, because you have done this thing, and have not withheld your son, your only son— [17] blessing I will bless you, and multiplying I will multiply your descendants as the stars of the heaven and as the sand which is on the seashore; and your descendants shall possess the gate of their enemies. [18] In your seed all the nations of the earth shall be blessed, because you have obeyed My voice." (Genesis 22:15-18)

Breathe, boo. With all the twists and turns, ups and downs of the process, frustration has had you in your feelings. I know; me too. It hasn't always been easy to discern the hand of God at work. We have felt downright crazy through this! More often than not it seemed like we took two baby steps forward only to be thrust back behind the starting line. Abraham thought he achieved the final victory only to be presented with the challenge of offering Isaac back to God. Feelings… seemed like… looked like… I thought.

Wait for it. Slowly, steadily, surely, the time approaches when the vision will be fulfilled. Discouragement wants to have its way. Instead, let faith arise. The sealing of the deal for Abraham was in proving to not only know God as Friend and Provider but also as Lord, the One to whom he was fully submitted. You see, the prize of the process isn't just the fulfilment of the promise; it is also the development of a surrendered heart. It is in the middle – the space of time between the hearing of the word and seeing the word come to pass – that we come to know Him as the Author and Finisher of our faith. Character development is built into the covenant. We serve a thorough God!

PROPULSION POINT: The end of the process provides an understanding of the process.

Discovery

Identify the Lie: All this wasn't even necessary.

Identify the Truth: Over time, the recesses of our hearts are revealed. The trusted Potter takes His time in working dead things out of us while kneading Life and Light into us. It is during the process that our hearts become purified and our faith is fortified.

And you shall remember that the LORD your God led you all the way these forty years in the wilderness, to humble you and test you, to know what was in your heart, whether you would keep His commandments or not. (Deuteronomy 8:2)

Declaration

Now thanks be to God who always leads us in triumph in Christ, and through us diffuses the fragrance of His knowledge in every place. (II Corinthians 2:14)

Hun—neeeey, we made it!!!

Listen, we've been keepin' it real all this time; no need to stop now. There is a possibility that you're still in process. That is perfectly okay! *Be not weary in well doing, for in due season you shall reap if you do not lose heart.* (Galatians 6:9). I'll let you in on a little secret – I'm actually in process while writing this. Wait! Before you throw the whole book away, hear me out. Processes come and go. Honestly, sometimes they even overlap. This isn't my first one and it definitely won't be my last. The same holds true for you. We go from glory to glory in this life of faith. Each new level is preceded by a new process.

I have seen the Word work on my behalf time and time again. I have partnered with countless others on their faith journeys to see the fulfillment of whatever "it" they trusted God to produce. Because of this, I have been able to confidently walk this road with you. Thank you for the privilege of doing so. Hear my heart when I say it is not taken lightly.

As we part ways, I pray that our assurance remains in God's consistency. He is the same yesterday, today, and forevermore. As He was with Abraham, so He is with you and me. If your process isn't over, wait for it. *Slowly, steadily, surely, the time approaches when the vision will be fulfilled.* Blessed is the one who yields to the process, for in doing so an inward work of completion produces an outward life of fullness.

Sincerely,

LaToya NaShae

About the Author

LaToya NaShae's passion and purpose are equipping others to live like they know WHOSE they are. This is accomplished through the avenues of writing, speaking, and coaching. She readily comes along beside others on their journey to discovering who they are in Christ and becoming empowered to walk in purpose. Whether publicly declaring the Good News of Christ or engaged in one-on-one coaching, LaToya walks with others along their journey of faith and freedom. Her aim is to encourage you to live an unstuck, unbound, unbreakable life in Christ!

LaToya NaShae is a graduate of Murray State University and Christian Coach Institute. She currently resides in Middle Tennessee where she serves as the founder and C.E.O. of BREAKOUT Coaching.

Bonding Through BREAKOUT

It is LaToya NaShae's sincere desire that every follower of Christ would live an unstuck, unbound, unbreakable life in Him. She encourages all who connect with her through social media to become a BREAKOUTER. What is that you ask? A BREAKOUTER is one who walks by faith and not by sight to reach an appointed place of purpose and promise. If this is you (or what you aspire to be) connect with the BREAKOUT crew by following LaToya NaShae.

Facebook   @Breakout-Coaching
Instagram   @coach_latoyanashae
YouTube   LaToya NaShae
Website   www.breakoutcoaching.buzz

Additional Notes

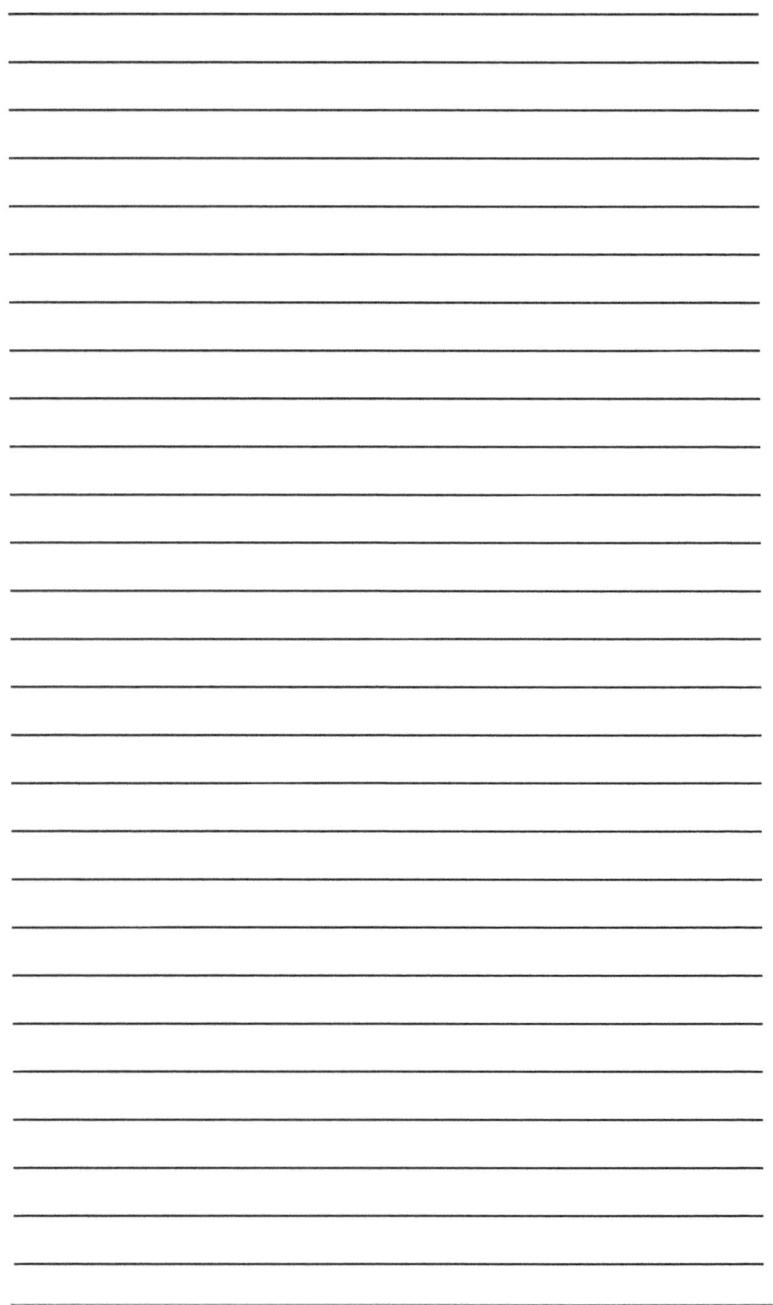

www.ingramcontent.com/pod-product-compliance
Lightning Source LLC
Chambersburg PA
CBHW021936040426
42448CB00008B/1093